DEMOCRACY AT WORK

A CITIZEN'S GUIDE

Published in the United States of America by Cherry Lake Publishing
Ann Arbor, Michigan
www.cherrylakepublishing.com

Content Adviser: Austin McCoy, Doctoral Candidate in History at the University of Michigan
Reading Adviser: Marla Conn MS, Ed., Literacy specialist, Read-Ability, Inc.

Photo Credits: © Dave Newman/Shutterstock, cover, 1; © Alison Hancock/Shutterstock, 5; © Joseph Sohm/Shutterstock, 6, 12; © Burlingham/Shutterstock, 8; © Rena Schild/Shutterstock, 11, 28; © Jason and Bonnie Grower/Shutterstock, 14; © mdgn/Shutterstock, 15; © Barry Blackburn/Shutterstock, 17; © Everett Collection/Shutterstock, 18; © Gyorgy Barna/Shutterstock, 20; © EdStock/istock, 21; © Martin Dallaire/Shutterstock, 23; © Rob Crandall/Shutterstock, 24; © Everett Historical/Shutterstock, 26

Library of Congress Cataloging-in-Publication Data
Names: Mara, Wil, author.
Title: Democracy at work / Wil Mara.
Description: Ann Arbor, Michigan : Cherry Lake Publishing, 2017. | Series: A
  citizen's guide | Includes bibliographical references and index.
Identifiers: LCCN 2016001519| ISBN 9781634710657 (hardcover) | ISBN 9781634711647
  (pdf) | ISBN 9781634712637 (pbk.) | ISBN 9781634713627 (ebook)
Subjects: LCSH: United States—Politics and government—Juvenile literature.
  | Separation of powers—United States—Juvenile literature. |
  Democracy—United States—Juvenile literature.
Classification: LCC JK40 .M36 2017 | DDC 320.473—dc23
LC record available at http://lccn.loc.gov/2016001519

Cherry Lake Publishing would like to acknowledge the work of the Partnership for 21st Century Learning.
Please visit *www.p21.org* for more information.

Printed in the United States of America
Corporate Graphics

ABOUT THE AUTHOR

Wil Mara is an award-winning and best-selling author of more than 150 books, many of which are educational titles for young readers. Further information about his work can be found at www.wilmara.com.

TABLE OF CONTENTS

CHAPTER 1

Democracy Then And Now

The United States of America is probably the most successful example of a **democracy** in human history. The foundation for that success lies in a document called the Constitution. You might think of it as America's **blueprint**. The terms of the Constitution were first debated in 1787 in Philadelphia, Pennsylvania, in the now-famous building known as Independence Hall. It is the very same place where the Founding Fathers forged another great document, the Declaration of Independence. This is why Philadelphia is often called the "Cradle of Liberty."

The United States is a known as a representative democracy. There are way too many of us to assemble in one place and discuss governmental matters, so we elect certain people to

The Constitution was signed at Independence Hall in Philadelphia, Pennsylvania.

Politicians often want to meet the people they will be representing.

represent our interests instead. They are known as **politicians**.
These people work in the various branches and levels of our
government. A mayor, for example, is a politician who runs a
local government, with local meaning the town or city in which
he or she lives. Then there are politicians at the state level, such as
a **governor**—the top politician in a state—and a lieutenant
governor, who is one step below the governor.

Finally, there is the federal government, which manages
issues affecting the entire country. The head of the federal
government is the president of the United States, and the person

just below the president is the vice president. As you might imagine, running the United States is a big job, and there are plenty of other people in the federal government who help the president get things done. All American citizens 18 or older have the right to vote in order to choose which people become politicians. Politicians are given a lot of power when they're voted into office, so the right to vote should be taken very seriously! You vote through a process called an **election**, where you go to a location near your home—usually called a **polling place**—and make your choices in private. This means you don't have to share your choices with anyone.

21st Century Content

England, the nation whose rule the American colonists escaped during the Revolutionary War (1775-1783), does not have a president at the head of its government. Instead it has a prime minister, who is elected by the people of the United Kingdom. The prime minister remains in power as long as he or she has support from House of Commons, which is the lower house of the British Parliament.

Voting is usually a private process.

Elections are held on a regular basis, depending on where you live and which political position is up for a vote. The election for president of the United States, for example, is held every four years (always in a leap year). Elections for a state's governor are also held every four years, but not necessarily in the same year as the presidential elections. Each state has a slightly different election cycle.

The men who wrote the Constitution and the Declaration of Independence wanted to make sure the government of the United States did not turn out like England's. England ruled America at the time, and the Founding Fathers thought that King George III was a tyrant. So they made sure no one person or governmental group had too much power. They did this by creating a government that has three main branches (sections): **executive**, **legislative**, and **judicial**. Each branch has certain powers that the other two do not. This system is often called **checks and balances**.

Life and Career Skills

Part of being a politician in the United States (or anywhere) means being good at choosing a certain point of view on an issue and then sticking to it. And in the world of politics, that means being challenged from time to time by people—including other politicians—who disagree with you. Politicians spend a lot of time debating their position on these issues, which means they have to believe strongly in them. Think about the things you feel strongly about. How far would you go to defend your beliefs? How sure are you that your beliefs are the right ones?

CHAPTER 2

The Executive Branch

The executive branch of the United States government oversees the daily administration of the country and carries out its laws. The top position in the executive branch is the president. It might sound like an illustrious position. After all, the president of the United States is one of the most powerful people in the world. But think of all the pressure and responsibility the job holds.

The president not only deals with the other two branches of government every day, but also manages America's relationship with all foreign governments. He or she is the "face" of America and has to maintain a good relationship with as many of its citizens as possible—even the ones who didn't vote for him or her.

Barack Obama was elected President in 2008.

President Bush speaks to military leaders at a parade in 1991.

He or she must have a good relationship with the media (journalists and photographers who work for television, radio, and the Internet). The president is also the commander in chief of America's **armed forces**. A critical part of the job is to keep America safe at all times. It's quite a job description!

The president also appoints many of the officials who help run the federal government. This is highly important, because many of these same officials oversee everything from the country's national parks and the military to **NASA** and the **FBI**. They control public health agencies such as the National

Institutes of Health and the Centers for Disease Control and Prevention. They administer the nation's mint, where our money is made, and the National Archives, where our Constitution is kept on display. All these responsibilities and many, many more begin right there in the famous Oval Office of the White House. That's where the president goes to work every day.

Life and Career Skills

*Another critical quality for an American president to have is the ability to make compromises. Whether a president likes it or not, there will always be people in power from the opposing political party. So, a Democratic president will have conflicts with Republicans from time to time. He won't get everything he wants just because he's the president. Imagine that the president wants to raise the nation's **minimum wage** by $3. Republicans may not be willing to go along with it unless they get some things in return. That may include a wage hike of only, say, $2.*

Vice President Joe Biden gives a speech.

The members of Congress meet in the Capitol Building.

21st Century Content

Many people think of the vice president (VP) as the second most powerful person in the U.S. government. After all, that position is just one step below the presidency, right? Wrong. In truth, the vice presidency has been viewed throughout history with bitterness and disdain, often by the people who have held the office! The VP has very little actual power. He or she cannot make or decide policy and cannot override the president on any political matter. The VP must have all comments cleared by the president's office first before making them to the media or public. However, he or she is the leader of the U.S. Senate. In a 50-50 tie, the VP is the deciding vote, which often means he or she could go ahead with what the president wants.

CHAPTER 3

The Legislative Branch

The legislative branch of the U.S. government is known as Congress. Like the other branches of government, Congress is located in the nation's capital of Washington, D.C. The core duty of Congress is to make new laws and sometimes adjust existing ones. That's why it's called the legislative branch: the word *legislation* means "the act of creating laws." Congress is divided into two parts, called chambers. One is called the Senate, and the other is the House of Representatives. Each state elects exactly two senators, which means there are 100 senators working every day in the Capitol, the building where Congress meets. The House of Representatives is a very different story. There are 435 representatives. Since there are 50 states in the country and 435 is

Virginia congressman Rob Wittman greets constituents.

not neatly divisible by 50, you might wonder how this can be. It's simple. The number of representatives from each state is determined by that state's population. Thus, the more people who live in a state, the more representatives it will have in the House of Representatives. Since Congress's primary role is to make new laws and adjust existing ones, let's take a quick look at how the process works.

First, members of Congress meet with citizens, various experts, and one another to find out what new laws might best

Congress spends a lot of time listening to ideas for new laws.

serve the nation's interests. They usually meet with the president, too. Only senators or representatives can get the process rolling, and it can begin in either the Senate or the House. The senator or representative first writes up what's called a bill. Both the House and the Senate have groups called committees, and the bill goes to whichever one is appropriate for the potential law in question. For example, if the bill is about farming, it goes to the Agriculture Committee. If the bill is about spending money, it goes to the Appropriations Committee.

Hearings are held by committees to see how the public feels

about the new law. These hearings may last from a few hours to a few days. Changes—known as **amendments**—will be made to the bill while the committee and the public discuss it. Often a bill will receive such a bad reaction that it stops and goes no further. This is commonly called being "killed in committee," and it happens more often than you might think. Thousands of bills are submitted by members of Congress every year, but only a tiny percentage become new laws.

If the committee agrees that a bill is good, it is sent back to the members of either the Senate or House (wherever it started). More amendments will likely be made, and then a vote is taken. If the vote is favorable, the bill is sent to the other chamber of Congress for further consideration (and usually more amendments). If that chamber votes in favor of the bill, it takes its final step: it goes to the president for approval or rejection. Approval means the president will sign the bill, and it will become a new law. If the president doesn't approve of it, the bill will be **vetoed**. *Veto* is a Latin word meaning "I forbid."

The vetoed bill goes back to Congress, where one of three things can happen. Congress can kill the bill altogether. It can change the reasons the president vetoed it and send it back to

The president can veto a bill if he or she doesn't agree with Congress.

Congress can overrule the president, but it doesn't happen very often.

him. Or Congress can go around the veto and pass the bill into law on their own. That last option isn't easy, however. Two-thirds of the members of Congress have to vote to approve the bill, and getting that many senators and representatives to defy a presidential veto can be very difficult. But it has happened, and there's no doubt it will happen again in the years ahead.

CHAPTER 4

The Judicial Branch

The third branch of the federal government is the judicial branch, also called the judiciary. Its central body is known as the Supreme Court, which is the highest and most powerful court in the nation.

The Supreme Court usually has nine members, each known as a **justice**. A justice is first appointed by the president. That appointment must be approved by the Senate. The Senate does not simply approve every person the president picks. The Senate holds hearings, and the person has to spend many tiring days answering questions from senators. Other people—both those in favor of the president's nominee and those who aren't—get the chance to speak their minds, too. This process can take several months. While that might sound a little over the top, consider

The Supreme Court is the most powerful court in the United States.

this: Supreme Court justices can hold this position for the rest of their lives! That's a lot of power and influence for one person to have over an entire nation. So the people who get that privilege need to be chosen very carefully.

The Supreme Court's job is to fairly and effectively interpret the laws that have been written for the United States. It's not an easy task. Justices have to basically understand what the creators of those laws had in mind when they created them. The process through which this happens takes the form of a court case. Lawyers on each side argue about the meaning

Each person on the Supreme Court goes through a long and difficult process before being chosen.

and intent of a certain law. The case must go through other courts first before it can get to the Supreme Court. Those courts are much lower in rank and power. They have to offer their opinions about the case first before anyone can ask the Supreme Court to get involved. The Supreme Court receives requests to hear thousands of cases every year. They agree to hear some, while most are rejected.

Supreme Court justices take their work very seriously, because their decisions can affect the lives of millions of Americans. They thoroughly study the details of each case and

21st Century Content

Today there are three women on the Supreme Court. The first to reach the post was Sandra Day O'Connor, who was appointed by President Ronald Reagan in 1981. The latest, Elena Kagan, was put on the court by President Barack Obama in 2010. There haven't always been women on the Supreme Court, but today girls can be proud of the trail blazed by these women and can work to reach the post themselves.

President Taft eventually was appointed to the Supreme Court in 1921.

then meet with one another to discuss a course of action. After enough research and discussion is done, the justices cast a vote on each case. The final decision is determined by the majority of the nine members: at least five justices have to agree on the outcome of the case. One justice will then write a report explaining the majority's decision. Other justices may write about the case, too. For example, if a vote is five to four, one of the justices in the minority group may feel the need to write an explanation about why he or she did not agree with the majority.

Life and Career Skills

William Howard Taft was the U.S. president from 1909 to 1913, after Theodore Roosevelt. He and Roosevelt were best friends for years. But Taft only did a so-so job of continuing Roosevelt's policies, and they fell out of touch. Taft didn't get re-elected for a second term. Instead, his career took a new path. Eight years after he left the presidency, he was appointed Chief Justice of the Supreme Court by President Warren G. Harding.

Before a big decision is announced, people often
wait outside the Supreme Court to celebrate or protest.

Sometimes the Supreme Court rules that an existing law does not conform with the spirit of America's Constitution. If the justices reach this decision, then that law will no longer be in effect. Congress may at that point decide to rewrite the law to fix the problem that the Supreme Court exposed. Congress has to go through all the legislative steps to do so, and the president has to sign the bill into law. It can be a long and difficult process, but it's also a system that has proven to work well over time. Remember, it's the system the Founding Fathers wanted in order to ensure an effective, working democracy!

21st Century Content

*Congress has tremendous power. For example, it is the only governing body that can declare war on another nation. The president can request this, but Congress has the power to deny it. Congress also defines all **monetary** policy in the country—everything from tax laws to the printing of physical **currency**. Congress can establish post offices, issue patents, borrow money on behalf of the nation, and expand or shrink the military.*

Think About It

Find one of the most important, high-profile, and maybe even controversial decisions that the Supreme Court has made in recent years. Now debate it with someone. Pick a side—probably the side that you feel most strongly about—and argue why that's the correct way to look at the issue. Then switch places with your fellow debater and argue it from the other side. You might be very surprised at how easily you can see both sides of an issue. And you will appreciate just how challenging it is for Supreme Court justices to make their decisions!

Congress's greatest authority is its ability to create, adjust, or even withdraw existing laws. This means they basically write the "rule book" that U.S. citizens have to follow. Let's say you had all of Congress's power for a day. What one law would you get rid of ? What one law would you create? Explain your thinking behind each of these decisions.

For More Information

BOOKS

Krull, Kathleen, and Anna DiVito (illustrator). *A Kid's Guide to America's Bill of Rights.* New York: HarperCollins, 2015.

Richmond, Benjamin. *What Are the Three Branches of Government? And Other Questions About the U.S. Constitution.* New York: Sterling, 2014.

Winter, Jonah, and Barry Blitt (illustrator). *The Founding Fathers! The Horse-Ridin', Fiddle-Playin', Book-Readin', Gun-Totin' Gentlemen Who Started America.* New York: Atheneum, 2015.

ON THE WEB

Congress for Kids—The Three Branches of Government
www.congressforkids.net/Constitution_threebranches.htm

Kids.gov—Government
https://kids.usa.gov/government/index.shtml

PBS Kids—The Democracy Project: President for a Day
http://pbskids.org/democracy/be-president/

GLOSSARY

amendments (uh-MEND-muhnts) changes made to a bill

armed forces (AHRMD FORS-iz) all the branches of the U.S. military, which includes the Army, Navy, Air Force, Marine Corps, and Coast Guard

blueprint (BLOO-print) a detailed plan of action

checks and balances (CHEKS AND BAL-uhns-iz) a system that allows each branch of government to amend or veto acts of another branch, to prevent any one branch from exerting too much power

currency (KUR-uhn-see) the form of money used in a country

democracy (dih-MAH-kruh-see) a form of government in which the people choose their leaders in elections

election (ih-LEK-shuhn) the act of choosing someone or deciding something by voting

executive (ig-ZEK-yuh-tiv) branch of the federal government that is headed by the president

FBI (EFF-BEE-EYE) the Federal Bureau of Investigation; a branch of the U.S. government that investigates crimes

governor (GUHV-ur-nur) the highest elected official of a U.S. state

judicial (joo-DISH-uhl) branch of the federal government that is made up of the court system

justice (JUHS-tis) a judge

legislative (LEJ-is-lay-tiv) branch of the federal government that is made up of Congress

minimum wage (MIN-uh-muhm WAYJ) the smallest amount of money that can legally be paid for work

monetary (MAH-nih-ter-ee) having to do with money

NASA (NAH-suh) the National Aeronautics and Space Administration; the government agency dealing with space exploration and research

politicians (pah-lih-TISH-uhnz) people who run for or hold a government office

polling place (POHL-ing plase) the place where votes are cast and recorded during an election

vetoed (VEE-tohd) refused approval

INDEX